400 FIFTH AVENUE

400 FIFTH AVENUE

A NEW GWATHMEY SIEGEL LANDMARK

FOREWORD
ROBERT SIEGEL

INTRODUCTION
PAUL GOLDBERGER

PHOTOGRAPHY
EVAN JOSEPH

EDITED BY
BRAD COLLINS

RIZZOLI
NEW YORK

New York · Paris · London · Milan

CONTENTS

FOREWORD

Charles Gwathmey and I formed our partnership in 1967 and over a 45-year period completed over 400 projects varying in scale and use from private residences, university buildings of all types, museums, corporate office buildings, and hospitality and residential towers. Throughout the many years of our architectural practice we collaborated across a common desk adjacent to a large pinup wall, discussing and sketching ideas for each of the projects which we shared with our staff for continued development until Charles passed away at the age of 71 due to cancer. 400 Fifth Avenue was one of the last projects Charles was able to work on.

Charles was a remarkable individual with an endearing personality, a great physical presence, and a commitment to design and detail that was evident in his approach to all aspects of life. He was a great communicator, very good listener, and patient collaborator eager to hear the thoughts of others. He was a natural educator and enjoyed the one-on-one interaction with clients.

The design challenge of 400 Fifth Avenue was to create a modern-day tall building that could provide continuity of the midrise massing and complexity of detail of neighboring historic landmark buildings that framed Fifth Avenue. We accomplished this by setting the tower portion back from the streets on a 10-story-high base building that aligned with the neighboring historic buildings. The base building was clad in limestone with deeply recessed openings and capped by a contemporary reinterpretation of a cornice element that provided continuity of the massing and sub details of the traditional neighboring buildings. The design of the tower element involved faceted window assemblies contained between vertical limestone-colored precast concrete piers that allow one to look down to Fifth Avenue and that animate the façade by reflecting light in an ever-changing way throughout the day; the detail creates a unique profile as it turns the corners. Capping the tower is an inverted tall crown of outward-angled textured stainless-steel panels that glow when illuminated at night and reinforce the tradition of iconic tops on New York City skyscrapers.

Over the years of our practice we had the opportunity to create noteworthy works of contemporary architecture while extending the positive characteristics of their historical context. Whig Hall at Princeton University was one of the earliest projects in which we inserted a new building within the restored, burned-out classical framework of one of the first buildings constructed at the University. Our expansion Annex and restoration of the Frank Lloyd Wright-designed Guggenheim Museum in New York City was a reverse strategy in which we created a framework, a gridded background building against which the design nuances of the original rotundas could be appreciated and which served to anchor the composition within its Fifth Avenue context. More recently the Soho Mews residential complex within the landmark Cast Iron district of lower Manhattan involved the development of a contemporary architectural vocabulary as a reinterpretation of the historical cast iron and glass vocabulary which extended the scale and reinforced the character of the neighborhood while maintaining its unique architectural presence.

The creative process related to 400 Fifth Avenue involved a wonderful collaboration with Davide Bizzi, of Bizzi and Partners Development, originally based in Milan, Italy, our client. Davide appreciated and supported the design efforts to create an iconic architectural solution using elegant materials and a density of details which distinguishes 400 Fifth Avenue from other recently designed tall buildings throughout New York City.

INTRODUCTION
PAUL GOLDBERGER

The name "Midtown South" does not evoke the kind of associations that many of New York's neighborhoods do: it is not known for its elegant town houses and apartment buildings, like the Upper East Side, or for its art galleries, like Chelsea; or for its cast-iron buildings, like SoHo, or for quaint blocks like the ones in Greenwich Village. It is not quite the theater district, which is a few blocks to the north, and it doesn't have the trendiness of the Flatiron and Union Square neighborhoods, which are just a few blocks to its south. It is, in some ways, an overlooked part of Manhattan, poised between the business and retail center of Midtown Manhattan and the gentrified precincts of the Flatiron district, its identity set mainly by the presence of one of the world's great landmarks, the Empire State Building, which since 1931 has presided over this part of the city with a breathtaking majesty. A neighborhood that has the Empire State Building, one is tempted to say, needs nothing else.

But in fact the neighborhood has plenty of other distinguished works of architecture: the sumptuous former home of the B. Altman & Co. department store, now the home of the Graduate Center of the City University of New York; the former Tiffany & Co. store by McKim, Mead and White, inspired by a Venetian palazzo; and the building that may be McKim's great masterpiece, the Morgan Library, now part of a larger museum complex designed by Renzo Piano. The northern boundary of Midtown South is marked by Raymond Hood's brilliantly composed, diminutive tower, the American Radiator Building, now the Bryant Park Hotel. And that building sits across the street from New York's greatest work of Beaux-Arts architecture, Carrère and Hastings's New York Public Library.

So this part of the city does not lack for landmarks. What the neighborhood has never had, however, has been another tall building of distinction. This is less a matter of architects and developers being intimidated by the presence of the Empire State Building, though that would be understandable, as it is a function of the marketplace: when the neighborhood developed as a commercial district, early in the twentieth century, the demand for skyscrapers was focused in the financial district of Lower Manhattan, and Midtown South developed mainly with buildings of less than a dozen floors. Fifth Avenue below 42nd Street was an elegant shopping street, not a place for tall towers. By the time the market was ready for skyscrapers in places other than Wall Street, the retail and office center of midtown had already moved farther to the north, leaping over Midtown South.

The Empire State Building was actually an outlier, the only very tall building for blocks around. It was built in 1931 on the site of one of the neighborhood's great landmarks, Henry Hardenbergh's original Waldorf-Astoria Hotel, itself built on the site of two mansions owned by the Astor family, which they sold when fashion dictated that the wealthy move farther uptown to escape the gradual crawl of commercial establishments up Fifth Avenue. That the Empire State was the only very tall building for blocks around enhanced its visibility to such an extent that protests were raised when a very tall and bulky office tower was proposed for a site two blocks to its west. The building deserves to stand alone, many people said. The view to the Empire State Building turned out to be as important to many New Yorkers as the view from it.

No such challenges were raised when 400 Fifth Avenue was proposed for a site even closer to the Empire State, just two short blocks to its north. But for good reason: 400 Fifth Avenue, by the architectural firm of

1

Gwathmey Siegel, is sophisticated, understated, and slender. It does not so much challenge the Empire State's supremacy on the skyline as it seeks to defer to it. And it marks the beginning of a new era for Midtown South, since this is the first building whose size and architectural quality, not to mention its tenancy, hold forth the possibility of redefining this portion of the city (1). The presence of the hotel and the 400 Fifth Avenue condominiums above it will, together, exert a new gravitational pull in the flux and flow of urban life in Manhattan, and will inevitably make this portion of Fifth Avenue no longer a valley between the center of midtown Manhattan and the Empire State Building, but a destination in itself.

Towers containing hotels and condominiums have been a common building form in the United States for at least a generation, but there are relatively few of them in New York, and fewer still designed by architects of note. It is a challenging building type for an architect, largely because so much is specified by functional demands: the hotel rooms need to be a certain size and layout, the condominiums generally require a different, equally specific size and layout, and there is only so much flexibility in the design of facilities like restaurants, spas, and fitness centers. Often the architect can exercise his or her hand mainly in the design of the façade, at least so far as visibility to the public is concerned, and even there, the shape of the building is likely to be predetermined by both functional demands and zoning laws, so designing the exterior becomes mainly a matter of creating a "skin," or sheathing for the tower.

The process of making architecture is, at bottom, a matter not of avoiding constraints but of being creative within them, not of denying constraints but of seeking ways to make them less limiting than they would otherwise appear to be. At 400 Fifth Avenue, Gwathmey Siegel faced no shortage of constraints. First, while the site is on New York's most famous avenue, it is also in a dense neighborhood with a somewhat discordant, not to say unruly, mixture of surrounding buildings, from the Empire State with its potential to overwhelm to gracious landmarks like the old Tiffany building to a number of nondescript commercial buildings with relatively honky-tonk retail stores on the ground floor. Second, the architects had to accommodate to the need to fit a certain number of condominium units and hotel rooms into a tight envelope. And third, they had to conform to zoning laws that called for a bulky 10-story base below a thinner tower.

The firm responded to these constraints with imagination and style, producing a building that surely ranks as its finest tower. Much of Charles Gwathmey and Robert Siegel's best work has been small in scale—houses, institutional buildings, and the like—and none of their most celebrated buildings, like Gwathmey's house for his parents on Long Island, or the DeMenil House, or several large villas in California, have been tall. Many of the tall buildings the firm has designed, such as the Morgan Stanley tower at 1585 Broadway and the condominium tower at Astor Place, both in New York, show an earnest attempt to rethink the form of a tall building in the center of the city, but they do not erase the sense that when all is said and done, these architects are more comfortable working at smaller scale.

But 400 Fifth Avenue suggests something entirely different: it is an inventive and beautiful exterior that, in and of itself, brings a powerful and serene architectural presence to what is, in the end, a relatively conventional shape. You sense that this time, the architects didn't try to fight the requirements that restricted them, but accepted them as constraints that come with building in the real world. And then they focused, intensely, on the part of the building that they could control, the design of the façade, and made of it something at once elegant, lively, and serene. Not the least of the values of 400 Fifth Avenue is the lesson it offers about picking your architectural battles, so to speak. Gwathmey Siegel didn't try to rethink the idea of the skyscraper, or of a combination hotel and condominium building; instead, the firm came up with a solution that accepted all the constraints it faced, and then proved how much creative leeway there could still be.

2

The base of the building holds to the even line of buildings on Fifth Avenue, reinforcing the street wall that is a key element to the urbanism of Fifth and most other New York streets, and meeting the cornice line of the old building to its north. At the southeast corner of the building, where it meets the corner of 36th Street, the base curves in a quarter-arc, a small gesture that at once enhances the corner and brings just enough change to the overall massing of the tower to create a sense of visual surprise, but not too much to disturb the integrity of the building as a strong, clear slab (2). It is an arc that serves, in a sense, as punctuation, and it also contains an entrance to the hotel's bar, which addresses the corner in a welcoming gesture. (The entrance to the hotel's lobby is directly on Fifth Avenue, under a metal canopy, to separate it clearly from the bar entry.)

Gwathmey Siegel's real creativity, however, was devoted to the skin itself, which is a mix of limestone, glass, and metal. The limestone covers the lower two floors, marking the public spaces of the hotel and strengthening the connection between the building and the older masonry buildings that are its neighbors. The windows are set deeply into the limestone, enhancing a sense of the base as a solid, heavy mass. The exterior gets thinner above, but it never takes on the extreme thinness of so many modern towers. The limestone continues vertically in between the windows, all the way to the top of the building, punctuated by a set of ridges at the midpoint of every floor, a subtle zig-zag in the limestone, Gwathmey Siegel's version of a traditional molding that adds depth and texture to the façade. The spandrels, the portions of the façade below the windows, are of metal, so the façade, in a sense, could be described as consisting of vertical stripes of limestone alternating with vertical stripes of metal and glass. If this can be viewed as paying homage to the Empire State Building, which is also sheathed in limestone with metal spandrels, it is the best kind of homage, loosely evocative without being a direct copy.

It is not the limestone or the metal that makes up the most striking element of the façade, however, but the glass, which projects out at a slight angle to the plane of the façade. In each room, there is a large panel of glass that tilts outward from top to bottom; below it is a smaller panel that tilts outward from the bottom, and the two meet to make

11

3

4

a horizontal line about two-and-a-half feet above the floor. The top panel is fixed; the lower one can be opened slightly as a casement, but the angle of both panels makes them seem, in effect, like casement windows in a partially open position.

It is a remarkable architectural detail, and it manages at once to bring a greater sense of space to the interior—the idea of a glass façade bulging out a few inches suggests a feeling of expansion that affects the tone of every room—and to create a lively, rhythmic texture on the façade. The angled panes of glass, covering the entire façade, along with the limestone moldings make this an unusually active façade for a modern building (3), with a sense of depth that is far from the sleek, flat façades of so many modern buildings, where any perception of depth is avoided and the goal is to make the exterior feel like the thinnest surface possible. At 400 Fifth Avenue, without using any traditional architectural elements, Gwathmey Siegel has created new versions of the very architectural elements—depth, texture, and solidity—whose absence from modern buildings is so often considered troubling.

The pattern of angled glass creates a particularly unusual detail at the corners of the building, where two sets of angled windows meet, which creates an exuberant projection of glass outward from the corner, enhancing the rhythm of the façade still further (4). The façade is also notable in the way in which it reflects light. When the condominiums were being sold, the sales staff referred to the windows as "diamond angle," and it is as good a term as any, since it underscores the sense that the entire façade is faceted. When the light reflects from one facet and not another, it enhances the sense of rhythm of the façade, and it becomes visually still richer. And as with all buildings that combine glass, metal, and stone, the limestone here serves as a counterpoint to the reflective surfaces, giving the building a feeling of solidity that never varies, however bright or dull the glass and metal may be, as well as a sense of connection to the surrounding cityscape.

At the top, the limestone stripes continue into a metal crown that splays out slightly, marking the building's crown. The splayed crown subtly echoes the angled glass below, and it allows the tower to meet the sky with just the right degree of exuberance. Perhaps more to the point, this crown is altogether distinct from the famous profile of the top of the Empire State Building, a virtual logo for New York that would be unthinkable to parody anywhere, let alone in its shadow. In the building's crown, as in its façade, Gwathmey Siegel figured out a modern way to achieve a traditional goal—in this case, giving a New York skyscraper a lively and engaging top that joins it to the chorus of New York tower tops—by using materials and elements from elsewhere in the façade, assembled differently.

The building has 184 condominium apartments, whose interiors were designed by DAS Concepts Inc. The goal was to echo the sense of modern luxury that the façade projects, and the design balances a sleek simplicity with a sense of richness. All of the units have open kitchens, with all of the cabinetry and appliances paneled in walnut, and like most newly designed condominiums in New York and elsewhere, the bathrooms are plentiful, large, and luxurious. The building has four exposures and every unit has a view of at least one portion of the Manhattan skyline. All of the units facing south have a close-in view of the Empire State Building in the foreground, a vista that no other building can duplicate (5).

The design of the residents' eleventh-floor roof deck, lounges, common spaces, and spa continues the same theme, as do the interiors of the hotel. In addition to the large bar area in the rounded corner, the hotel has a high lobby facing Fifth Avenue and a second-floor restaurant; the hotel guest rooms, like these spaces, are also modern and discreetly elegant, extending the sense of understated modern luxury of the condominiums. The building is all of a piece from its base to its crown: a modernist gem in which Gwathmey Siegel shows that a new tower can be built on a challenging site in the center of a challenging city, and fit neatly into its surroundings while still breaking new architectural ground.

5

Gwathmey Siegel has created new versions of the very architectural elements—depth, texture, and solidity—whose absence from modern buildings is so often considered troubling.

Looking east on 42nd Street

Situated in a section of New York's fabled Fifth Avenue that connects two celebrated urban neighborhoods, 400 Fifth Avenue works to make this a destination in its own right. Landmarks to the north include the Public Library, the Chrysler Building, Rockefeller Center, Grand Central Terminal, and St. Patrick's Cathedral. To the south are the Flatiron Building, Madison Square Park, and the marble arch of Washington Square. To the immediate west is the garment district.

Despite being bracketed by such venerated design icons, the stretch of Fifth Avenue from 23rd Street to 42nd Street has its own distinguished architectural heritage. A variety of Beaux-Arts buildings from the art deco period lining the thoroughfare here are testimony to the city's northward development in the early twentieth century when fashionable retail buildings began to replace the churches, clubs, and residences that had originally occupied it. Commercial buildings designed in the Italian palazzo style with refined decorative detailing and gracious arcade windows began to signal this area of Fifth Avenue as a premier mercantile boulevard. At Fifth Avenue and 36th Street is the stately limestone and granite Gorham Building designed in 1903 by McKim Mead & White in the Florentine Renaissance style for the silver manufacturing company. Even more notable a block north is Stanford White's Tiffany Building with its more lavish embellishment and modeling; not long after the building's completion in 1906, Architectural Record magazine declared it "frivolous" in comparison to the more sedate Gorham Building. Despite such critical rebuke, the white marble retail emporium remained the home of the celebrated jeweler until its final move uptown to 57th Street in 1940.

Numerous other commercial buildings in the immediate area, some also landmarked historic structures, all work to establish an energetic horizontal rhythm on this area of Fifth Avenue. Towering above them all is the Empire State Building, the 102-story skyscraper of limestone, steel, and glass. Built in the art deco style and completed in 1931, it is a landmark not only of architecture and design but of the progressive thinking and soaring aspirations of American culture and economy of that period.

The challenge, then, was to create a large tower composition in a neighborhood of smaller landmark buildings. Developer and architect were also charged with enhancing the neighborhood and introducing a higher level of street vitality. Thus the tower nods to the design heritage surrounding it, all the while establishing a new standard in contemporary architecture for the area. Both sympathetic to its historic site and expressive of early-twenty-first-century urban design, 400 Fifth Avenue contributes to the design legacy of this area.

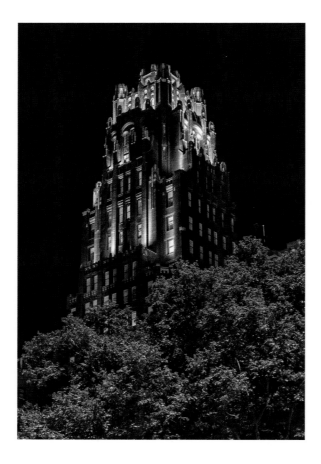

Looking north to Grand Central Station

. . . the tower nods to the design heritage surrounding it, all the while establishing a new standard in contemporary architecture for the area.

Tiffany Building (previous spread) | The Ansonia Hotel | Corner of Fifth Avenue and 36th Street looking toward Gorham Building

THE BUILDING

While the 600-foot-tall building generously references classical skyscraper design, it is not at the expense of a contemporary sensibility. In purchasing the air rights from McKim, Mead & White's landmarked Tiffany Building across the street, Bizzi & Partners Development participated in New York City's landmarks transfer program: in exchange for the air rights, the developers allowed the Landmarks Commission the right to review its design; to assess both how the new building acknowledges the adjacent properties and how it relates to the particular landmark building whose air rights it was using; and perhaps, most important, to demand a level of quality in return to the community. Such considerations are routine at Bizzi. The firm's development protocol includes recognizing emerging neighborhoods; leveraging the value of existing historic areas; and advancing them through the distinguished architecture and design of its own properties.

Equally driven by the imperative to advance the site, Gwathmey Siegel is a natural partner for the project. Adhering to a philosophy that includes a respect for both location and historic precedent, the firm's renown rests on its simultaneous commitment to modernism and sensitivity to site. Confronting difficult and complex locations and entering into full engagement with the Landmarks Commission has distinguished its previous buildings in New York City. As Robert Siegel observes, "Contextuality helps to make a place more of a place. Our intent is to design buildings that enhance what is there, while remaining fresh in their own right."

Certainly 400 Fifth Avenue does both these things. Attuned to context, the 60-story luxury hotel and residential tower observes Louis Sullivan's classical tripartite scheme of base, shaft, and cap. The 10-story base of the building, or podium, is clad in limestone and remains consistent in scale and design with existing buildings in that area of Fifth Avenue; the column covers accentuating the building's shaft express urban verticality; and the inverted crown capping the building brings a new silhouette to the midtown skyline.

The exterior rhythms of the building take their cues from landmarked buildings immediately around them, including the Empire State Building's vertical column covers situated between double bay windows split by mullions. The Indiana limestone used for the podium is similar in tone and texture to the limestone used both for the Empire State Building and for the Gorham Building to the immediate south. And the generously scaled street-level arcade windows, stone spandrels, and double cornice banding at the podium reference similar features on the Tiffany Building on Fifth Avenue at 37th Street. Even the building's radiused corner at 36th Street, while completely modern in articulation, observes historic precedent. A number of heralded historic buildings in the neighborhood from the nineteenth and early twentieth centuries, most markedly the Flatiron Building, have such rounded corners, which are more hospitable than sharp edges both to the eye and to the flow of pedestrian traffic.

All that said, the limestone, steel, and glass building is clearly of the twenty-first century. The carved volumes and depth of recesses in the façade give the building a sense of depth that is not the norm in contemporary architecture, and full-height, faceted windows especially give the building modern dimension.

In an elegant response to building code mandate that habitable rooms in residences and hotels have natural light and ventilation, traditional bay windows have been rotated 90 degrees to become vertical. Lower sections of the windows are fully operable, offering guests and residents a unique view to the streetscape below and allowing them the ultimate luxury of fresh air.

The profiled pre-cast concrete of the façade breaks down the scale of the building; it adds a bit of decorative detail and interacts visually with the surface texture of the faceted windows. And while it may be a sympathetic nod to the neighboring historic structures, its restraint is also consistent with the crisp grid of the façade.

Textured stainless-steel panels with horizontal ribbing floating upward between the concrete columns at the building's cap form a screen wall that conceals mechanical systems and elevator bulkheads. Especially when uplit in the evening, the outward angle of the crown brings a distinguished new profile to Manhattan's midtown skyline. All of which allows the building to speak eloquently to its own time as well.

. . . the outward angle of the crown brings a distinguished new profile to Manhattan's midtown skyline.

And while it may be a sympathetic nod to the neighboring historic structures, its restraint is also consistent with the crisp grid of the façade.

View from Fifth Avenue (previous spread) | Views from southeast corner of Fifth Avenue and 36th Street

THE HOTEL

That the hotel sets out to be an urban retreat is clear at the entrance, where the revolving glass door is articulated as a transparent cylindrical volume with a glass wall. Continuing the strict angularity of the building and geometry of the steel entrance canopy, the lobby area is a convergence of clean modernism and warm refuge.

Symmetrical and ordered, the recessed entry is on axis with the elevators, flanked at the north by the concierge desk and at the south by the reception desk. At ground level the building is exposed from one end to the other, creating a layered sense of spaciousness.

The lobby has been opened up with a long, lateral axis to the bar, a strategy that takes the eye along the corridor through a glass wall to the staircase and beyond. The reception area between the main axis of the lobby and the street provides a sense of spatial release both vertically to the double height space overhead and horizontally out to the street. A bronze mirror and backlit gold onyx reception desk cast a welcoming glow across the entrance area. Fumed oak paneling with a subtle matte finish and polished limestone floors suggest a level of craftsmanship that adds to an atmosphere of haven.

Mediating this space is the fluid form of the elliptical limestone staircase leading to the restaurant on the floor above. A sculptural gesture that is simultaneously refined and exuberant, it animates not only the lobby, but the exterior of the building as well. Positioned as a counterpoint to the rectilinear space, its fluid form is underscored by the interplay between its exterior glass rail and interior fumed oak rail. Hanging within its helix is Santiago Villanueva's *Falling White*, a glistening lacquered teardrop that highlights the sense of suspension created by the floating steps.

Elsewhere in the lobby, artwork is testimony to Manhattan's role as one of the world's premier art meccas. The mannequins that greet visitors at the entrance by folk artist Mark Perry offer a figurative riff on the tailors' dummies that populate the neighboring garment district, while Anne Moran's iridescent tapestry of patinated copper fragments behind the reception desk is a more abstract composition.

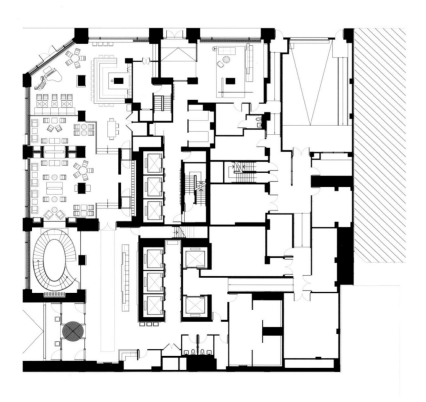

Reception toward stair and *Falling White* | Entry to bar | First-floor plan

The honed limestone corridor of the lobby continues down two steps and directly into the Bar, and the change in elevation indicates the shift in function from the private hotel lobby to a more public gathering space. There, a rectilinear bar, columns, and marble counters re-establish the clear grid of interior space. The scale of the grid, however, varies to create a lively rhythm. In the immediate bar area, a counter of black marble, dark walnut floors, and muted upholstery create an elegant sanctuary. Elsewhere, column lines create discrete spaces. Built-in shelves and cabinetry in fumed oak and columns sheathed in olive fabric, along with marble-topped bar tables and subdued lighting, make for a subtle, cosmopolitan feel. A rug in varied chocolate stripes, plush corner couches, wingback chairs, leather banquettes and bar stools, and a fireplace all suggest the quiet comfort and luxury of a traditional men's club. Zoning mandated that this ground-floor area serve as a retail space; thus the bar, accessible through its own corner street entrance, is open to the public.

A subdued lighting plan reinforces the intimate atmosphere; recessed, low-profile fixtures highlight numerous seating groups. Lighting is focused on the bar tables themselves, with the areas around them darker. And because the fixtures are adjustable, seating arrangements remain flexible. In the evening, subtle perimeter accent lighting at the windows shimmers with the sheer draperies, while linear light strips at the bar and wall shelves cast soft illumination without obvious sources. Lighting in the cabinetry millwork highlights a carefully curated collection of glasswork, ceramics, and books. The result is a space that manages to glow with minimal intrusion from the light sources themselves.

As in the lobby, the use of smoked mirrored surfaces works both to enlarge the space and to reinforce the idea that the urban landscape—whether in the curtain walls of skyscrapers, storefront windows, or bright signage—is a place of constant reflection. Sheer window treatments in a neutral hue put guests at a subtle remove from the unceasing hum of street life just outside. Indeed, the sensibility of a serene retreat is in counterpoint to the vivid, visual cacophony of the cityscape just beyond the wide display windows, where the constant stream of pedestrian traffic and the flow of bright yellow cabs animate the urban stage that is lower Fifth Avenue.

Bar detail (previous spread) | Bar toward corner entry

Bar toward lobby | Seating with *Falling White* beyond (following spread)

Lobby sitting area with bar beyond | Stair and *Falling White* | Reception from stair (following spread)   77

Positioned as a counterpoint to the rectilinear space, its fluid form is underscored by the interplay between its exterior glass rail and interior fumed oak rail.

Detail of stair | Stair toward restaurant entry

The vertical sinuous curve of the stair terminates at the glazed entrance to the hotel's restaurant—Michael White's Ai Fiori. Immediately inside is a 25-foot white marble bar, leather stools, and mirrored ceiling that establish a tone of urban sophistication. To the left is the dining room; to the right is a curved, continuous banquette that defines the fluid space accommodating additional bar seating.

The relaxed and familiar sensibility of the bar gives way to greater formality in the restaurant. While its name translates to "Among the Flowers," the restaurant is more cosmopolitan than pastoral. Use of the column line and an L-shaped plan break up the space to create a series of smaller, private dining areas. A floor striped with black oak and a lighter Brazilian cherry establishes a lively graphic rhythm, while panels of sheer drapery diffuse the light from the wide windows without compromising the views to Fifth Avenue. A composition of highlights and lowlights illuminates the space. Architectural lighting can be aimed at the dining tables. Because there are few banquettes, tables can be moved for a variety of configurations, with lighting adjusted accordingly. Small table lamps are used as well both to suggest a residential, romantic atmosphere and to bring down the scale of the space. The spacious main dining room seats 165, while two more intimate private dining rooms accommodate 12 and 20 guests.

Columns have been wrapped in a chenille-like fabric that both softens the room and reduces sound levels. The pale aqua used on the walls is suggestive of sea and sky, and oversize photographs on the wall display impressionistic images of Portofino and Cinque Terre—picturesque fishing villages and resort towns on the Italian Riviera, the locale that has also inspired the menu. Along with wood paneling, the rustic earthtones used for the upholstery and interior finishes and vast sculptural flower arrangements collaborate to evoke a modern Mediterranean atmosphere.

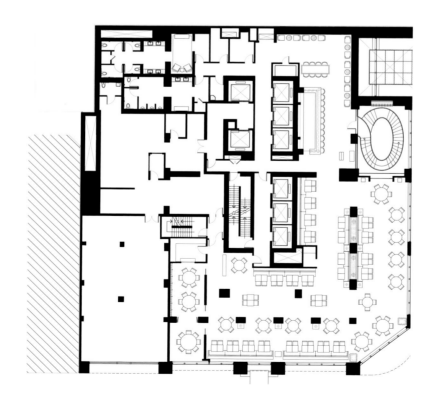

Dining room | Second-floor plan | Dining room

Spaciou

The Ulti

Luxury

isness

mate

THE ROOMS

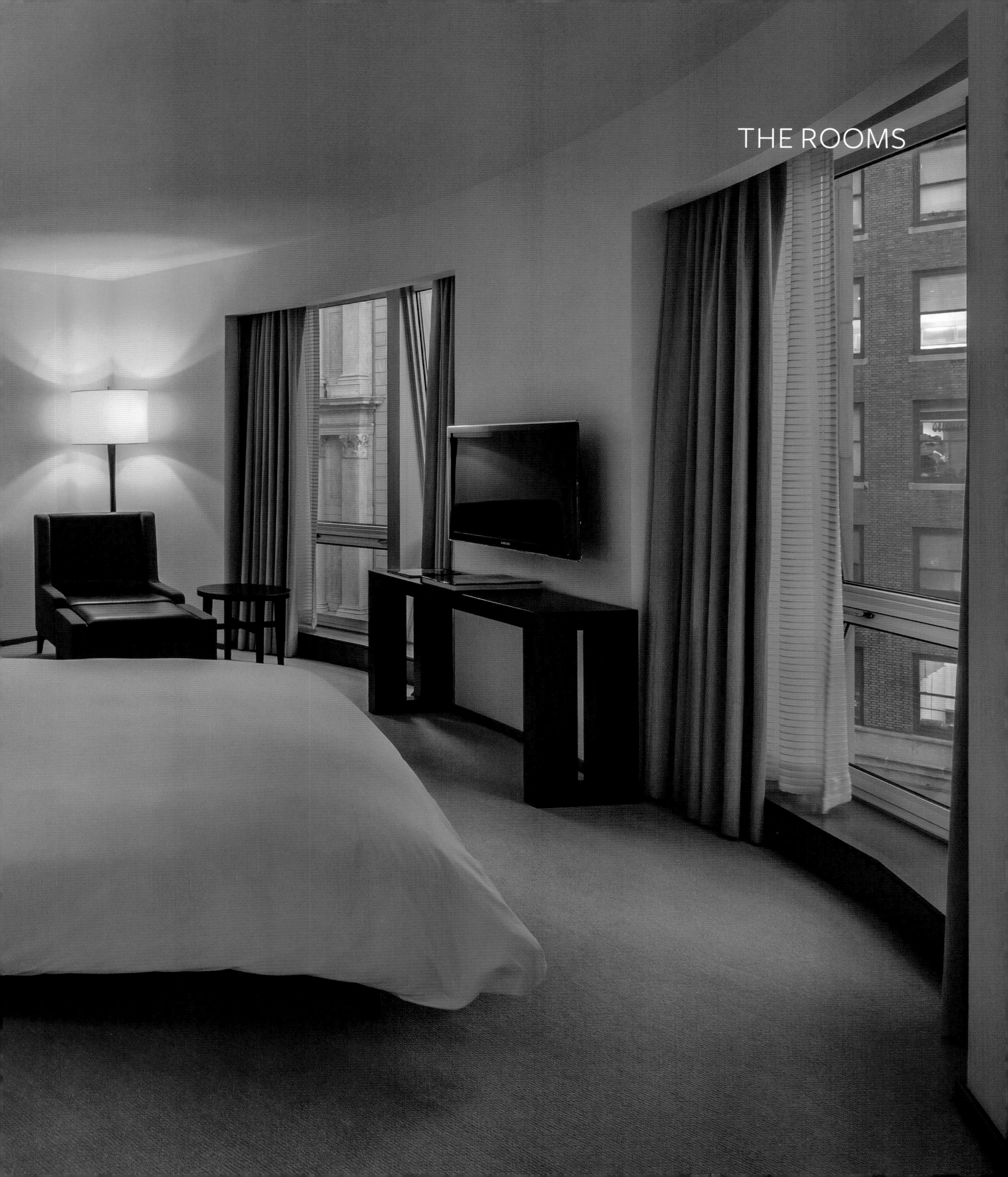

Writing area with bedroom beyond (Deluxe Room)

The character of luxury is often specific to place. In Manhattan, then, where space is at a premium, it is defined by spaciousness. The 157 guestrooms and 57 suites are all distinguished by their generous dimensions: guestrooms average at 800 square feet, while suites are anything from 1,100 to 4,000 square feet. In an era of micro hotels and ever-diminishing scale in the hospitality industry, such expansiveness is a genuine hallmark of luxury.

Walnut floors and a foyer of built-in walnut cabinetry lead guests to the sleeping area. Throughout the guestrooms, palette is muted, decoration limited. Whether in shelving, counters, or desks, fine woodworking integrates interior design elements with architecture whenever possible, eliminating the need for superfluous objects and embellishments. Guest rooms are largely self-decorating, with their furnishings working in counterpoint to the frame of the room. Furniture systems have been assimilated into the paneled walls, establishing a visual and functional continuity that is its own amenity.

While guestrooms have over 25 different floorplans, largely determined by architectural floor plates, these generally conform to one of several configurations. On the eleventh floor and above, where the floorplate is smaller, beds are positioned facing the windows, with the bathroom located between the bed and corridor. Here, panels that open behind the bed allow natural light into the bathroom. If the distance between the elevator shaft and building perimeter is too short for this layout, rooms may have the bed parallel to the windows, with the bathroom also sited at the perimeter windows. When the distance is greater, as in those rooms directly overlooking Fifth Avenue on the fifth through tenth floors, bathrooms and closets are located toward the rear, with beds positioned facing the window. Seating and work areas are located near the windows, with wood flooring indicating change in use.

Flooded with natural light, nearly all the rooms and suites offer expansive views. With operable lower panels that allow for fresh air, the floor-to-ceiling faceted windows also suggest that the art is the surrounding urban landscape. Observing the premise that guests should know what city they are in, the designers use the view to midtown and beyond to bring the city into the building. Two layers of window treatments—a sheer fabric that filters sunlight and views to the rooms and a heavier black-out drapery—allow for both natural illumination and maximum darkness. Equally spacious bathrooms, some as large as 12 by 15 square feet, have full-height windows that offer the same panoramic vistas as the sleeping areas. Pale Calcutta marble floors and walls, along with deep soaking tubs and frameless glass shower doors, confirm the intersection of rigorous modernism and indulgent sensuality, a hallmark of the work of both Gwathmey Siegel and DAS Concepts.

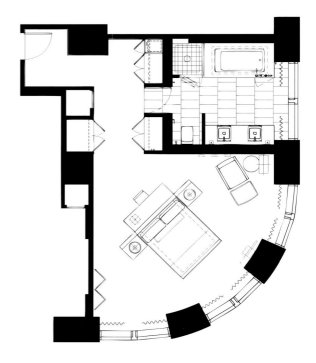

Sitting area from bedroom | Sitting area with desk

Furniture systems have been assimilated into the paneled walls, establishing a visual and functional continuity that is its own amenity.

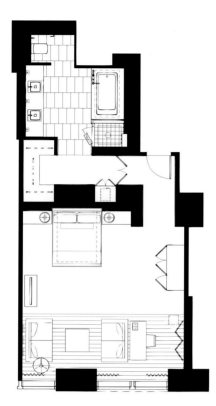

Sitting area from kitchen (previous spread) | Kitchen and sitting area toward bedroom

In an era of micro hotels and ever-diminishing scale in the hospitality industry, such expansiveness is a genuine hallmark of luxury.

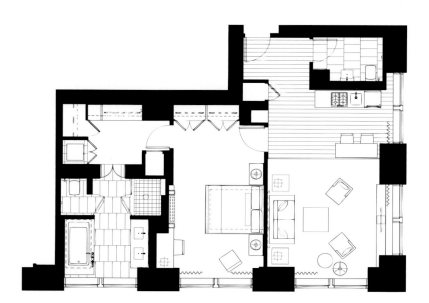

Details of headboard wall with sliding panels

Sitting area (previous spread) | Sitting area toward kitchen

With operable lower panels that allow for fresh air, the floor-to-ceiling faceted windows also suggest that the art is the surrounding urban landscape.

An Atmo
of Indul
Tranqui

osphere

gent

lity

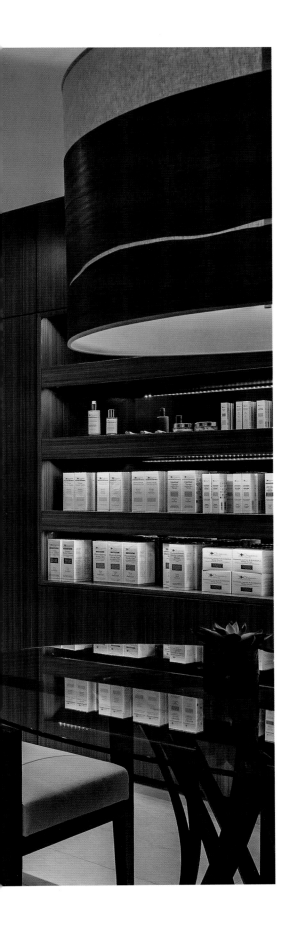

If 400 Fifth Avenue sets out to offer quiet sanctuary in the urban landscape, it is the 12,000-square-foot spa and fitness center that does this most explicitly. Occupying the entire fourth floor of the hotel, its interior of marble, polished limestone, Italian glass tiles, and walnut cabinetry establishes an atmosphere of indulgent tranquility. But it is water that remains the predominant theme here, and what most defines the space are all those ways with which the varied levels and rhythms of light—whether in frosted low-mounted wall lights or flickering colored ceiling panels—interact with water, steam, and ice. With an aqua lounge, rain showers, steam rooms, plunge pool, and ice cave, the spa oasis fully demonstrates the restorative qualities of water and light.

When possible, natural light from the perimeter windows flood the treatment rooms. In the steam bath that takes its cues from a traditional Turkish hamam, sparkling pinpoints of LED lights work to recreate the effect of natural daylight. Translucent wall panels, surface tiles in iridescent Italian glass, and marble benches further refract the light. Near the soaking tub, soft candlelight creates a quiet, soothing atmosphere. And in the experiential showers, colors morph in an illuminated overhead panel—from soft oranges and pinks to blues and greens—while music plays as well. Down the hallway, the more austere ice room with cooler overhead lighting has been surfaced in small glass tiles suggestive of tiny cubes of ice. Despite such variations in illumination, levels of lighting are kept low and soft to suggest an environment of soothing serenity.

Men's changing room detail

But it is water that remains the predominant theme here, and what most defines the space are all those ways with which the varied levels and rhythms of light—whether in frosted low-mounted wall lights or flickering colored ceiling panels—interact with water, steam, and ice.

Crisp
Contem
Aesthet

nporary
ic

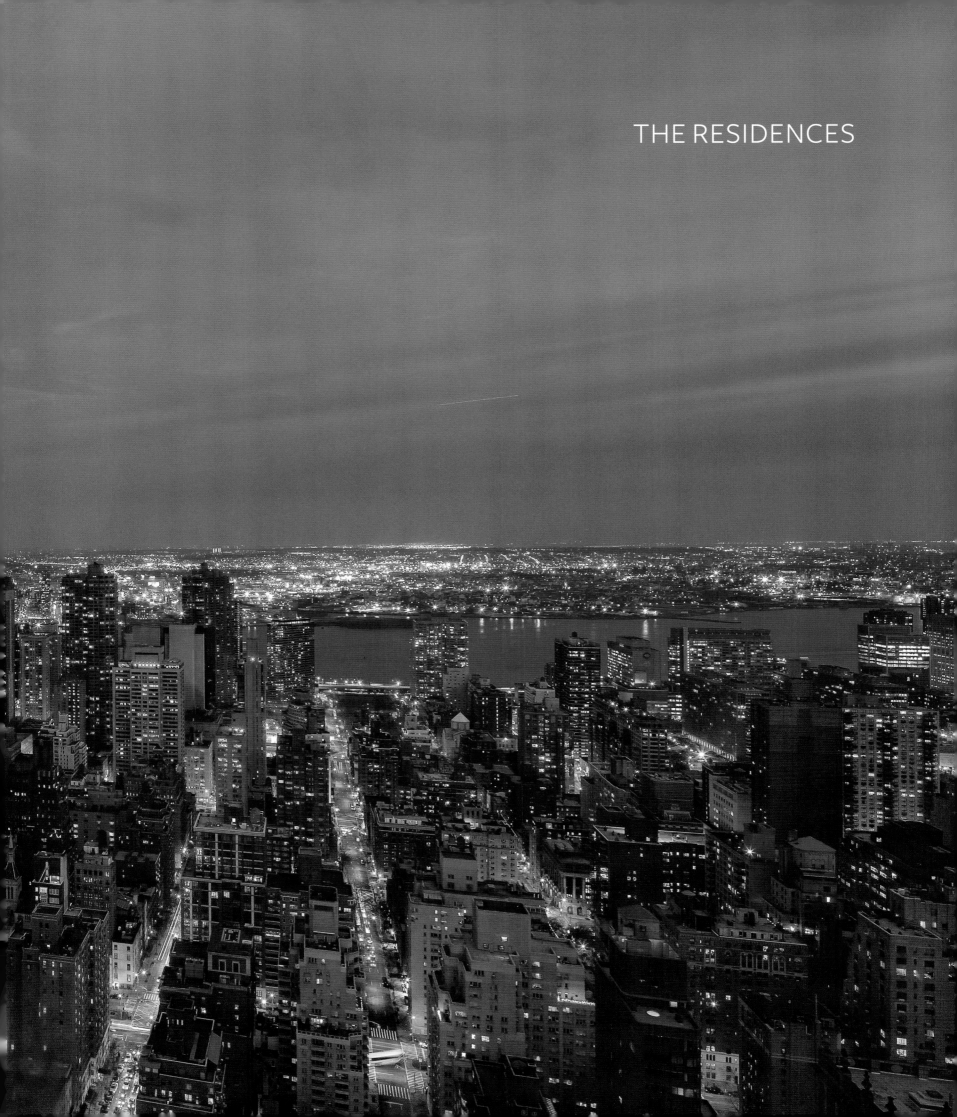

THE RESIDENCES

A separate entrance takes residents to the 184 private apartments located on the 31st to 60th floors of the tower. With a backlit gold onyx reception desk, subdued lighting, a polished gray limestone column, and an art deco–style laser-cut steel screen that gives texture and dimension to the intimate space, the small foyer is a discreet entry to the residences above.

At the 31st floor, precast concrete exterior corner columns have been eliminated, and the full-length faceted windows wrap the corners of the building to create the atmosphere of an urban aerie. Such faceting allows residents to actually view the street beneath them, conferring a dramatic—and authentic—sense of height. More importantly, perhaps, it reflects different planes of light throughout the day, animating the interior space. If the windows bring texture to the exterior of the building, what they bring to the interior is a kinetic energy. Visitors may well imagine they are afloat in the city skyscape. Hand-laid black oak hardwood floors, built-in walnut cabinetry, stone countertops, and clean lines are the components of seamless interiors and continue the crisp contemporary aesthetic established elsewhere in the building. Materials and fixtures specified for bathrooms—Haisa marble flooring and countertops, Zuma soaking tubs, frameless glass shower doors, and rainfall showerheads—further advance the convergence of luxury and modernism.

While the floorplan and design of the residences provide an envelope for limitless possibilities, a series of showcase apartments suggests particular directions these possibilities may take. In one apartment by designer Nicole Fuller, a variety of metal finishes exploits the extravagant light of the tower apartment. A recessed metal mesh screen with an antiqued brass finish functions as a veil separating living area from the kitchen. Add to that a mid-century brass lamp over the sectional sofa, a birch log pattern in metallic foil pressed into the wallpaper behind it, brass accents on the leather counter stools, and hammered polished nickel lamps in the kitchen and the entire space is a symphony of reflective surfaces and accents. Elsewhere, more subtle devices have been used to play with light, such as the metallic silver threads woven into the soft linen drapes in the master bedroom. All of these elements allow the residence to make the most of both the natural daylight and sparkling evening illumination of the cityscape beyond.

A second apartment by Phoebe and James Michael Howard is distinguished by casual elegance and traditional comfort. In the living area, a small sofa has been placed at an angle to the windows to animate the rectangular space. The ceiling, painted a pale sage green and varnished, shimmers at night. And in the master bedroom, icy grays and silvery blues provide a soothing, restful palette while referencing the skyline just outside the window. In a child's room, a sculpted valance and canopy over the bed both make for a sense of retreat and add height to the room.

And in yet another apartment designed by Richard Hallberg for a Wall Street financier, a black and white palette transforms the subdued, contemporary interior to an elegant gallery for a varied collection of art and antiquities that ranges from Han Pottery and a Renaissance line drawing to an Alexander Calder mobile and a painting by Takashi Murakami. No less eclectic, furnishings include gilt sconces, a gold-leafed coffee table, a bronze bench, and a steel console. While only three variations, these interiors indeed attest to the broad range of design expression the tower residences can accommodate.

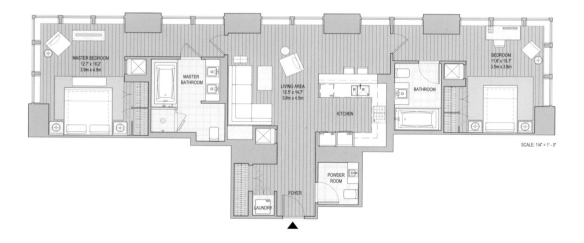

Master bedroom and bath (previous spreads) | Bedroom

Reconn
to the C

ecting

ity

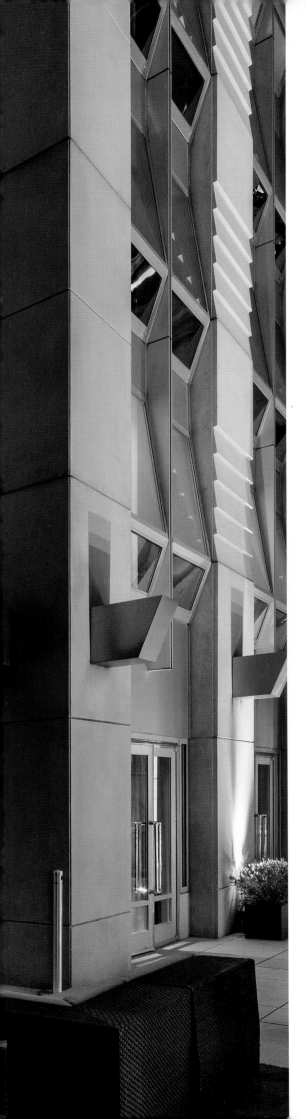

A precise geometric layout confers a sense of quiet order on the residential terrace that takes advantage of the building's setback on the 11th floor. Wrapping the building on three sides, the secluded sky garden offers residents an outdoor room with ample views to the Empire State Building two blocks south. Square cut-outs in the limestone frame views to the surrounding cityscape, in some cases providing a concise surround for a vignette of the lavishly modeled columns and cornices of the historic buildings just beyond. In warmer weather, a quiet stream of water in a terrace fountain makes for calming acoustics. While limestone floor and walls continue the material used on the building's exterior, low evergreen trees that keep their color year-round, potted orchids, and a crisp patch of lawn all offer a natural respite from the hardscaping of the urban environment.

The interior lounge includes a pool table room with a quartz bar, leather barstools, and built-in walnut cabinetry. A sitting room at the other end is equipped with a flatscreen TV, a couch, and armchairs. Walnut cabinetry, a gas fireplace, and a granite hearth add to the sense of comfort and warmth. Two additional gas fireplaces outdoors allow the entire area to be used even in cooler weather. With doors that can be opened or closed and furniture that can be easily moved, the flexible space can serve as a single, large flowing room or as a series of several smaller, more intimate chambers.

View into interior of lounge | Exterior of curved terrace corner   193

Terrace fountain and sitting area

Square cut-outs in the limestone frame views to the surrounding cityscape, in some cases providing a concise surround for a vignette of the lavishly modeled columns and cornices of the historic buildings just beyond.

Detail of terrace with the Empire State Building beyond | View toward private residential terraces

Terrace looking west | Billiard room

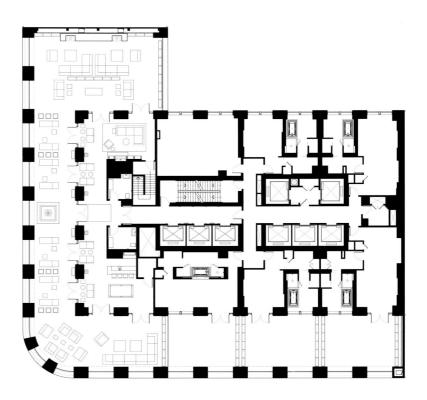

Media room (previous spread) | Southwest corner of terrace with fireplace and the Empire State Building beyond

Terrace detail with Gorham Building beyond 205

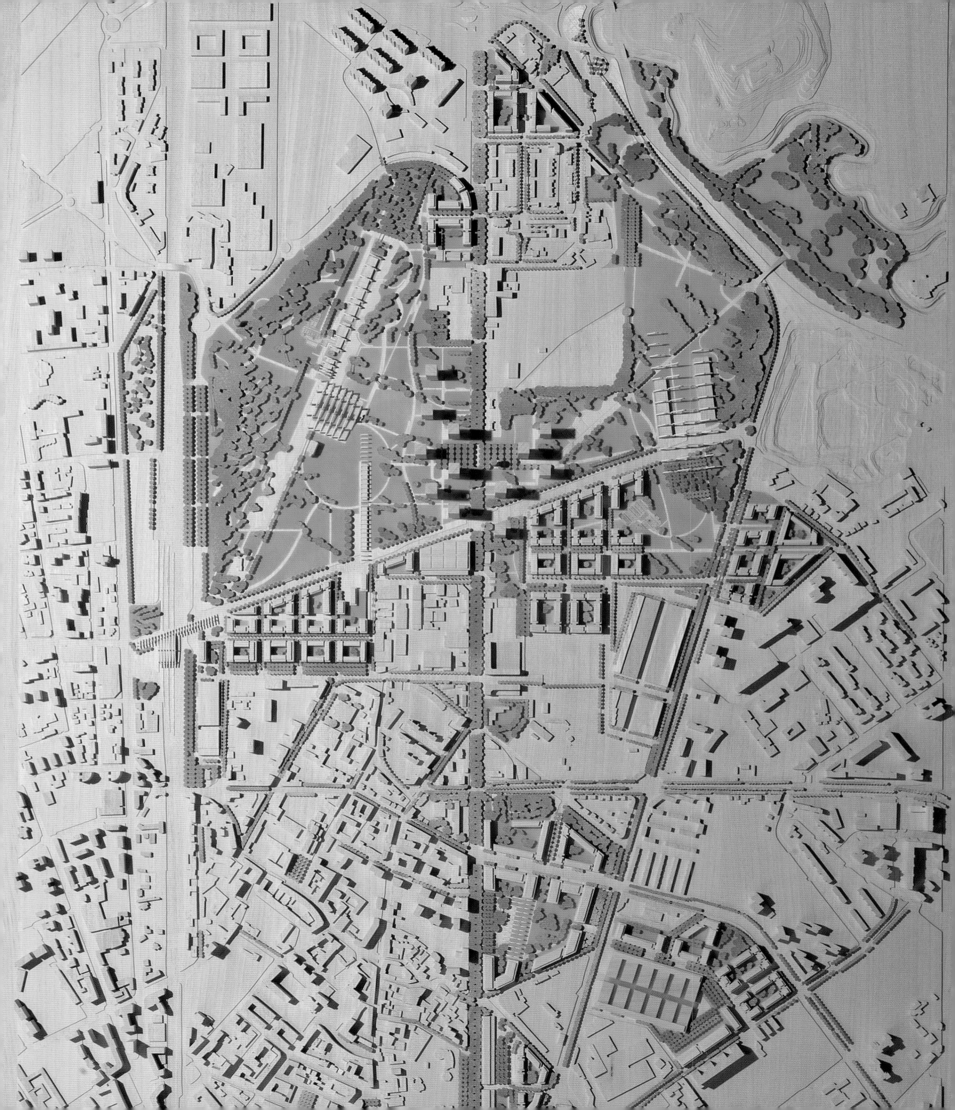

BIZZI & PARTNERS DEVELOPMENT

While 400 Fifth Avenue may be a new landmark on lower Fifth Avenue, the tower also stands for an innovative alliance between concerns. Which is to say, the project speaks to the value of a strong and mutually sympathetic relationship between developer, architect, and interior design firm. The partnerships with Gwathmey Siegel and DAS Concepts were opportunities for Bizzi & Partners to confirm its commitment both to design excellence and to making a decisive economic and design impact on the locations of all its properties.

Bizzi & Partners Development is a global real estate firm whose reputation has been forged by such partnerships. And as demonstrated by the collaborative efforts here, the commitment to develop properties that optimize the economic opportunities of their locations is achieved through alliances with internationally renowned architects and designers. Among the other landmark buildings around the world that are an outcome of this strategy: Milanosesto, a 145-hectare, mixed-use project outside of Milan designed by Renzo Piano that adheres to standards of sustainability while fully acknowledging the historic industrial buildings nearby; two 39-story residential towers of Estrela do Atlantico, designed by Abreu/Barros in Natal, Brazil, that signal an emerging region in Latin America; and the renovation of the historic Hotel Angst in the Italian Riviera in a restoration program that includes both the celebrated buildings and their once lavish botanical gardens. The firm's intensive approach to development gives broad consideration to local historic and artistic values and environmental principles; maintaining high aesthetic standards and adhering to the economic demands of the communities in which it operates are dual imperatives.

Bizzi & Partners is focused on the development of premier commercial and residential properties in Europe, North America, and South America. The firm is led by an executive team with decades of experience in real estate development, including the acquisition, financing, construction, and renovation of a wide array of property types. Real estate professionals managed by this team are responsible for all aspects of project management. The firm's senior management has considerable experience in developing properties throughout the world with specific expertise in foreign real estate emerging markets. As a global concern with offices in Milan, New York City, Tallinn, and São Paulo, Bizzi & Partners Development has developed and marketed more than 20 million square feet of space comprised of residential, retail, office, and parking uses.

GWATHMEY SIEGEL & ASSOCIATES ARCHITECTS

If 400 Fifth Avenue is a twenty-first-century building that expresses generous acknowledgment of its twentieth-century neighbors, such sensitivity is the hallmark of the work of Gwathmey Siegel & Associates Architects. Recognizing a building's contextual setting, whether historic or contemporary, has distinguished the firm's work from its inception, and numerous buildings in New York's urban landscape reflect the graceful rationale of such an approach. Uptown, Gwathmey Siegel's addition to the Guggenheim Museum in the early 1990s added more than 65,000 square feet of space. While recognizing the grandeur of the original Frank Lloyd Wright rotunda, the addition also anchored it against a unifying frame. Downtown, the curvilinear glass Astor Place, while contemporary in form and material, nonetheless engages the adjacent historic Cooper Square; situated as a floating rotational object in a vector of streets, the building employs the older masonry buildings around it as a stabilizing surround. And in the immediate midtown area of 400 Fifth Avenue, the firm had renovated B. Altmans, a department store built in the neoclassical style, to accommodate a graduate center for the City University of New York. The exterior of the landmarked building was left largely intact, though the interior was transformed to become a contemporary vertical campus with classrooms, lecture halls, an auditorium, recital hall, theater, TV studio, gallery, and conference center.

The value of this approach has been confirmed by more than 100 design awards, continuing recognition in the professional and general press, and inclusion in exhibitions and histories of contemporary architecture. In 1982, Gwathmey Siegel & Associates received the American Institute of Architects's highest honor, the Firm Award for "approaching every project with a fresh eye, a meticulous attention to detail, a keen appreciation for environmental and economic concerns, and a strong belief in collaborative effort." This collaborative strategy applies not only to the company's client relationships, but also to its internal creative and project management process, as well as its working relationships with consultants and specialists.

With over 400 projects completed for educational, healthcare, corporate, cultural, government, and private clients throughout the United States and abroad, the New York based firm has an international reputation for architectural excellence. Charles Gwathmey passed away on August 3, 2009, after battling cancer for several years. The firm's leadership continues to be provided by principal and founding partner Robert Siegel and Gene Kaufman, who joined the firm in 2011. The two partners are involved in all phases of the design process of every project, whether in master planning, architectural, interior, or product design services.

DAS CONCEPTS

400 Fifth Avenue was designed with the goal of giving guests and residents the quintessential New York experience, while also offering haven and respite. The use of rich, natural materials, a varied art collection, the suggestion that the views to the urban streetscape animate the building's interiors, and, above all, a serene sense of comfort distinguish both public and private spaces of the building. The approach that luxury can be particular to place reflects DAS Concepts's philosophy of hospitality design: each commission is viewed as an opportunity to create integrated environments that reflect both the spirit of their locale and the culture of the client, and that are beautiful, effective, and functional. Such a philosophy that allows each project to develop its own character has earned principal Don Siembieda *Interior Magazine's* "Best Hotel Design Award" for the Four Seasons Hotel in New York and the James Beard Award for the 5757 restaurant, also at the Four Seasons hotel.

Though a young and dynamic interior design firm, DAS Concepts has a long pedigree in hospitality and hotel design, and principals Don Siembieda and Francisco Jové bring their clients a combined experience of over 50 years in the design arena. The firm is distinguished by its depth of knowledge in the design of hotel properties; its spirit of collaboration with the other team members; its uncompromised attention to detail; its concern for craft; and its comprehensive understanding of the value added by good and pertinent design. Both principals are actively involved in the development of all projects and promote an environment that fosters creativity, personal growth, and responsibility and integrates the views of all team members in the decision-making process.

With offices in Long Beach, California, DAS has developed a body of work that represents some of the most innovative and unique luxury hotel properties around the world, including those in Shanghai, Tokyo, São Paulo, Goa, and Bermuda.

All photography, except images listed below
© Evan Joseph

First published in the United States of America in 2013 by
Rizzoli International Publications, Inc.
300 Park Avenue South
New York, NY 10010
www.rizzoliusa.com

ISBN: 978-0-8478-4122-6
LCCN: 2013941338

© 2013 Rizzoli International Publications, Inc.
Foreword © 2013 Robert Siegel
Introduction © 2013 Paul Goldberger

Designed by Group C Inc.

Distributed to the U.S. trade by Random House, New York

Printed and bound in China

2013 2014 2015 2016 2017 / 10 9 8 7 6 5 4 3 2 1